TRANSFORMATIONS

Also by Anne Sexton

POETRY

To Bedlam and Part Way Back   1960

All My Pretty Ones   1962

Live or Die   1966

Love Poems   1969

Transformations   1971

The Book of Folly   1972

The Death Notebooks   1974

The Awful Rowing Toward God   1975

45 Mercy Street   1976

Word for Dr. Y.: Uncollected Poems   1978

The Complete Poems   1981

Selected Poems of Anne Sexton   1988

PROSE

Anne Sexton: A Self-Portrait in Letters   1977

TRANSFORMATIONS

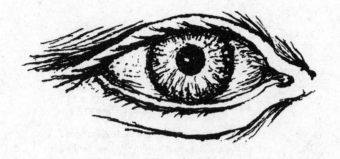

Anne Sexton

With a Foreword by Kurt Vonnegut, Jr.

Drawings by Barbara Swan

A Mariner Book

HOUGHTON MIFFLIN COMPANY

Boston • *New York*

First Mariner Books edition 2001

www.hmhco.com

ISBN 0-618-08343-X (pbk)
ISBN 978-0-618-08343-5 (pbk)

Library of Congress Catalog Card Number 71-156489

Printed in the United States of America

DOC 30 29 28 27 26
4500788591

Some of the poems in this volume have previously
appeared in the following magazines: *Audience*: "Iron Hans"
and "The Maiden Without Hands"; *Cosmopolitan*:
"Snow White and the Seven Dwarfs" and "Hansel and
Gretel"; *Playboy*: "The Little Peasant"

To Linda,
who reads Hesse
and drinks clam chowder

FOREWORD

by Kurt Vonnegut, Jr.

"Death starts like a dream, full of objects and my sister's laughter," Anne Sexton says in another book. "We are young," she goes on, "and we are walking and picking wild blueberries all the way to Damariscotta."

God love her.

. .

I asked a poet friend one time what it was that poets did, and he thought awhile, and then he told me, "They extend the language." I thought that was neat, but it didn't make me grateful in my bones for poets. Language extenders I can take or leave alone.

Anne Sexton does a deeper favor for me: she domesticates my terror, examines it and describes it, teaches it some tricks which will amuse me, then lets it gallop wild in my forest once more.

She does this for herself, too, I assume. Good for her.

. .

I don't know her well. I met her at a party for Dan Wakefield, a mutual friend. Dan had just published a novel about the tacky and bleak love life of a young man in Indianapolis after the Korean war. She had written a lot of love poems, I knew. One of them began like this:

This is the key to it.
This is the key to everything.
Preciously.

I am worse than the gamekeeper's children,
Picking for dust and bread.
Here I am drumming up perfume.

Let me go down on your carpet,
your straw mattress — whatever's at hand
because the child in me is dying, dying.

It is not that I am cattle to be eaten.
It is not that I am some sort of street.
But your hands found me like an architect.

Jugful of milk! It was yours years ago
when I lived in the valley of my bones,
bones dumb in the swamp. Little playthings.

And so on. There wasn't any woman as alive and appreciative as all that in Dan's book about Indianapolis. I, too, was from Indianapolis.

Indianapolis, by the way, is the world's largest city not on a navigable waterway.

. .

So I tried to be delightful to Anne Sexton, and a lover of life (which I'm not), and I drew for her this diagram of the story of Cinderella:

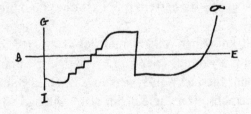

"G" was good fortune. "I" was ill fortune. "B" was beginning. "E" was end. Cinderella was low at the start. She sank even lower when her rotten stepsisters went to the party and she stayed home.

Then her fairy godmother appeared, gave her a dress and glass slippers and a carriage and all that. The steps in my chart represented those donations of valuable merchandise. Cinderella went to the party, danced with the prince. She crashed at midnight, but she wasn't as low as she used to be — because she remembered the party.

Then the glass slipper fit her, and she married the prince. She became infinitely happy forever — which includes now.

.   .

And I learn just now from an encyclopedia, which my wife bought volume by volume from a supermarket, that I graphed the English version of the story, which was translated from Charles Perrault's telling of it in French.

I learn something more from the encyclopedia, and I would have enchanted Anne Sexton and everybody at the party with it, if only I'd known: in the process of translation, the word *vair* was mistaken for *verre* so that Cinderella's fur slippers became glass.

So much for lucky poetry.

.   .

Anne Sexton found it kinky that I should tell her about Cinderella, since she was then absorbed by a darker, queerer version of that story — by the Brothers Grimm. She was, in fact, retelling many of the Grimms' fairy tales in poetry.

And here they are.

So much for mental telepathy. So much for new friends.

. .

How do I explain these poems? Not at all. I quit teaching in colleges because it seemed so criminal to explain works of art. The crisis in my teaching career came, in fact, when I faced an audience which expected me to explain *Dubliners* by James Joyce.

I was game. I'd read the book. But when I opened my big mouth, no sounds came out.

CONTENTS

TRANSFORMATIONS

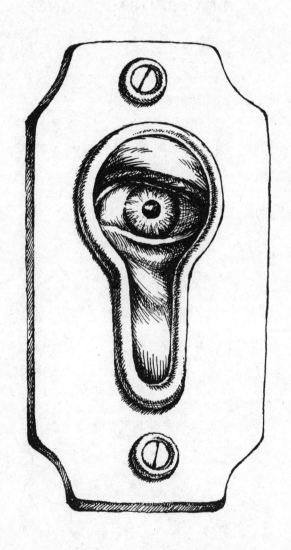

THE GOLD KEY

The speaker in this case
is a middle-aged witch, me —
tangled on my two great arms,
my face in a book
and my mouth wide,
ready to tell you a story or two.
I have come to remind you,
all of you:
Alice, Samuel, Kurt, Eleanor,
Jane, Brian, Maryel,
all of you draw near.
Alice,
at fifty-six do you remember?
Do you remember when you
were read to as a child?
Samuel,
at twenty-two have you forgotten?
Forgotten the ten P.M. dreams
where the wicked king
went up in smoke?
Are you comatose?
Are you undersea?

Attention,
my dears,
let me present to you this boy.
He is sixteen and he wants some answers.
He is each of us.
I mean you.
I mean me.
It is not enough to read Hesse
and drink clam chowder
we must have the answers.
The boy has found a gold key
and he is looking for what it will open.
This boy!
Upon finding a nickel
he would look for a wallet.
This boy!
Upon finding a string
he would look for a harp.
Therefore he holds the key tightly.
Its secrets whimper
like a dog in heat.
He turns the key.
Presto!
It opens this book of odd tales
which transform the Brothers Grimm.
Transform?
As if an enlarged paper clip
could be a piece of sculpture.
(And it could.)

SNOW WHITE
AND THE SEVEN DWARFS

No matter what life you lead
the virgin is a lovely number:
cheeks as fragile as cigarette paper,
arms and legs made of Limoges,
lips like Vin Du Rhône,
rolling her china-blue doll eyes
open and shut.
Open to say,
Good Day Mama,
and shut for the thrust
of the unicorn.
She is unsoiled.
She is as white as a bonefish.

Once there was a lovely virgin
called Snow White.
Say she was thirteen.
Her stepmother,
a beauty in her own right,
though eaten, of course, by age,
would hear of no beauty surpassing her own.
Beauty is a simple passion,

but, oh my friends, in the end
you will dance the fire dance in iron shoes.
The stepmother had a mirror to which she referred —
something like the weather forecast —
a mirror that proclaimed
the one beauty of the land.
She would ask,
Looking glass upon the wall,
who is fairest of us all?
And the mirror would reply,
You are fairest of us all.
Pride pumped in her like poison.

Suddenly one day the mirror replied,
Queen, you are full fair, 'tis true,
but Snow White is fairer than you.
Until that moment Snow White
had been no more important
than a dust mouse under the bed.
But now the queen saw brown spots on her hand
and four whiskers over her lip
so she condemned Snow White
to be hacked to death.
Bring me her heart, she said to the hunter,
and I will salt it and eat it.
The hunter, however, let his prisoner go
and brought a boar's heart back to the castle.
The queen chewed it up like a cube steak.
Now I am fairest, she said,
lapping her slim white fingers.

Snow White walked in the wildwood
for weeks and weeks.
At each turn there were twenty doorways
and at each stood a hungry wolf,
his tongue lolling out like a worm.
The birds called out lewdly,
talking like pink parrots,
and the snakes hung down in loops,
each a noose for her sweet white neck.
On the seventh week
she came to the seventh mountain
and there she found the dwarf house.
It was as droll as a honeymoon cottage
and completely equipped with
seven beds, seven chairs, seven forks
and seven chamber pots.
Snow White ate seven chicken livers
and lay down, at last, to sleep.

The dwarfs, those little hot dogs,
walked three times around Snow White,
the sleeping virgin. They were wise
and wattled like small czars.
Yes. It's a good omen,
they said, and will bring us luck.
They stood on tiptoes to watch
Snow White wake up. She told them
about the mirror and the killer-queen
and they asked her to stay and keep house.
Beware of your stepmother,

they said.
Soon she will know you are here.
While we are away in the mines
during the day, you must not
open the door.

Looking glass upon the wall . . .
The mirror told
and so the queen dressed herself in rags
and went out like a peddler to trap Snow White.
She went across seven mountains.
She came to the dwarf house
and Snow White opened the door
and bought a bit of lacing.
The queen fastened it tightly
around her bodice,
as tight as an Ace bandage,
so tight that Snow White swooned.
She lay on the floor, a plucked daisy.
When the dwarfs came home they undid the lace
and she revived miraculously.
She was as full of life as soda pop.
Beware of your stepmother,
they said.
She will try once more.

Looking glass upon the wall . . .
Once more the mirror told
and once more the queen dressed in rags
and once more Snow White opened the door.

This time she bought a poison comb,
a curved eight-inch scorpion,
and put it in her hair and swooned again.
The dwarfs returned and took out the comb
and she revived miraculously.
She opened her eyes as wide as Orphan Annie.
Beware, beware, they said,
but the mirror told,
the queen came,
Snow White, the dumb bunny,
opened the door
and she bit into a poison apple
and fell down for the final time.
When the dwarfs returned
they undid her bodice,
they looked for a comb,
but it did no good.
Though they washed her with wine
and rubbed her with butter
it was to no avail.
She lay as still as a gold piece.

The seven dwarfs could not bring themselves
to bury her in the black ground
so they made a glass coffin
and set it upon the seventh mountain
so that all who passed by
could peek in upon her beauty.
A prince came one June day
and would not budge.

He stayed so long his hair turned green
and still he would not leave.
The dwarfs took pity upon him
and gave him the glass Snow White —
its doll's eyes shut forever —
to keep in his far-off castle.
As the prince's men carried the coffin
they stumbled and dropped it
and the chunk of apple flew out
of her throat and she woke up miraculously.

And thus Snow White became the prince's bride.
The wicked queen was invited to the wedding feast
and when she arrived there were
red-hot iron shoes,
in the manner of red-hot roller skates,
clamped upon her feet.
First your toes will smoke
and then your heels will turn black
and you will fry upward like a frog,
she was told.
And so she danced until she was dead,
a subterranean figure,
her tongue flicking in and out
like a gas jet.
Meanwhile Snow White held court,
rolling her china-blue doll eyes open and shut
and sometimes referring to her mirror
as women do.

THE WHITE SNAKE

There was a day
when all the animals talked to me.
Ten birds at my window saying,
Throw us some seeds,
Dame Sexton,
or we will shrink.
The worms in my son's fishing pail
said, It is chilly!
It is chilly on our way to the hook!
The dog in his innocence
commented in his clumsy voice,
Maybe you're wrong, good Mother,
maybe they're not *real* wars.
And then I knew that the voice
of the spirits had been let in —
as intense as an epileptic aura —
and that no longer would I sing
alone.

In an old time
there was a king as wise as a dictionary.
Each night at supper

a secret dish was brought to him,
a secret dish that kept him wise.
His servant,
who had won no roses before,
thought to lift the lid one night
and take a forbidden look.
There sat a white snake.
The servant thought, Why not?
and took a bite.
It was a furtive weed,
oiled and brooding
and desirably slim.
I have eaten the white snake!
Not a whisker on it! he cried.
Because of the white snake
he heard the animals
in all their voices speak.
Thus the aura came over him.
He was inside.
He had walked into a building
with no exit.
From all sides
the animals spoke up like puppets.
A cold sweat broke out on his upper lip
for now he was wise.

Because he was wise
he found the queen's lost ring
diddling around in a duck's belly
and was thus rewarded with a horse

and a little cash for traveling.
On his way
the fish in the weeds
were drowning on air
and he plunked them back in
and the fish covered him with promises.
On his way
the army ants in the road pleaded for mercy.
Step on us not!
And he rode around them
and the ants covered him with promises.
On his way
the gallow birds asked for food
so he killed his horse to give them lunch.
They sucked the blood up like whiskey
and covered him with promises.

At the next town
the local princess was having a contest.
A common way for princesses to marry.
Fifty men had perished,
gargling the sea like soup.
Still, the servant was stage-struck.
Nail me to the masthead, if you will,
and make a dance all around me.
Put on the gramophone and dance at my ankles.
But the princess smiled like warm milk
and merely dropped her ring into the sea.
If he could not find it, he would die;
die trapped in the sea machine.

The fish, however, remembered
and gave him the ring.
But the princess, ever woman,
said it wasn't enough.
She scattered ten bags of grain in the yard
and commanded him to pick them up by daybreak.
The ants remembered
and carried them in like mailmen.
The princess, ever Eve,
said it wasn't enough
and sent him out to find the apple of life.
He set forth into the forest for two years
where the monkeys jabbered, those trolls,
with their wine-colored underbellies.
They did not make a pathway for him.
The pheasants, those archbishops,
avoided him and the turtles
kept their expressive heads inside.
He was prepared for death
when the gallow birds remembered
and dropped that apple on his head.

He returned to the princess
saying, I am but a traveling man
but here is what you hunger for.
The apple was as smooth as oilskin
and when she took a bite
it was as sweet and crisp as the moon.
Their bodies met over such a dish.
His tongue lay in her mouth

as delicately as the white snake.
They played house, little charmers,
exceptionally well.
So, of course,
they were placed in a box
and painted identically blue
and thus passed their days
living happily ever after —
a kind of coffin,
a kind of blue funk.
Is it not?

RUMPELSTILTSKIN

Inside many of us
is a small old man
who wants to get out.
No bigger than a two-year-old
whom you'd call lamb chop
yet this one is old and malformed.
His head is okay
but the rest of him wasn't Sanforized.
He is a monster of despair.
He is all decay.
He speaks up as tiny as an earphone
with Truman's asexual voice:
I am your dwarf.
I am the enemy within.
I am the boss of your dreams.
No. I am not the law in your mind,
the grandfather of watchfulness.
I am the law of your members,
the kindred of blackness and impulse.
See. Your hand shakes.
It is not palsy or booze.
It is your Doppelgänger

trying to get out.
Beware . . . Beware . . .

There once was a miller
with a daughter as lovely as a grape.
He told the king that she could
spin gold out of common straw.
The king summoned the girl
and locked her in a room full of straw
and told her to spin it into gold
or she would die like a criminal.
Poor grape with no one to pick.
Luscious and round and sleek.
Poor thing.
To die and never see Brooklyn.

She wept,
of course, huge aquamarine tears.
The door opened and in popped a dwarf.
He was as ugly as a wart.
Little thing, what are you? she cried.
With his tiny no-sex voice he replied:
I am a dwarf.
I have been exhibited on Bond Street
and no child will ever call me Papa.
I have no private life.
If I'm in my cups
the whole town knows by breakfast
and no child will ever call me Papa.
I am eighteen inches high.

I am no bigger than a partridge.
I am your evil eye
and no child will ever call me Papa.
Stop this Papa foolishness,
she cried. Can you perhaps
spin straw into gold?
Yes indeed, he said,
that I can do.
He spun the straw into gold
and she gave him her necklace
as a small reward.
When the king saw what she had done
he put her in a bigger room of straw
and threatened death once more.
Again she cried.
Again the dwarf came.
Again he spun the straw into gold.
She gave him her ring
as a small reward.
The king put her in an even bigger room
but this time he promised
to marry her if she succeeded.
Again she cried.
Again the dwarf came.
But she had nothing to give him.
Without a reward the dwarf would not spin.
He was on the scent of something bigger.
He was a regular bird dog.
Give me your first-born
and I will spin.

She thought: Piffle!
He is a silly little man.
And so she agreed.
So he did the trick.
Gold as good as Fort Knox.

The king married her
and within a year
a son was born.
He was like most new babies,
as ugly as an artichoke
but the queen thought him a pearl.
She gave him her dumb lactation,
delicate, trembling, hidden,
warm, etc.
And then the dwarf appeared
to claim his prize.
Indeed! I have become a papa!
cried the little man.
She offered him all the kingdom
but he wanted only this —
a living thing
to call his own.
And being mortal
who can blame him?

The queen cried two pails of sea water.
She was as persistent
as a Jehovah's Witness.
And the dwarf took pity.

He said: I will give you
three days to guess my name
and if you cannot do it
I will collect your child.
The queen sent messengers
throughout the land to find names
of the most unusual sort.
When he appeared the next day
she asked: Melchior?
Balthazar?
But each time the dwarf replied:
No! No! That's not my name.
The next day she asked:
Spindleshanks? Spiderlegs?
But it was still no-no.
On the third day the messenger
came back with a strange story.
He told her:
As I came around the corner of the wood
where the fox says good night to the hare
I saw a little house with a fire
burning in front of it.
Around that fire a ridiculous little man
was leaping on one leg and singing:
Today I bake.
Tomorrow I brew my beer.
The next day the queen's only child will be mine.
Not even the census taker knows
that Rumpelstiltskin is my name . . .
The queen was delighted.

She had the name!
Her breath blew bubbles.

When the dwarf returned
she called out:
Is your name by any chance Rumpelstiltskin?
He cried: The devil told you that!
He stamped his right foot into the ground
and sank in up to his waist.
Then he tore himself in two.
Somewhat like a split broiler.
He laid his two sides down on the floor,
one part soft as a woman,
one part a barbed hook,
one part papa,
one part Doppelgänger.

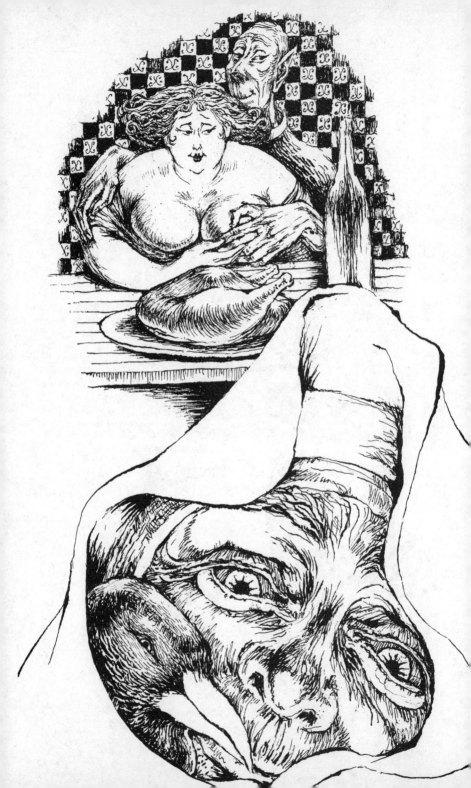

THE LITTLE PEASANT

Oh how the women
grip and stretch
fainting on the horn.

The men and women
cry to each other.
Touch me,
my pancake,
and make me young.
And thus
like many of us,
the parson
and the miller's wife
lie down in sin.

The women cry,
Come, my fox,
heal me.
I am chalk white
with middle age
so wear me threadbare,
wear me down,

wear me out.
Lick me clean,
as clean as an almond.

The men cry,
Come, my lily,
my fringy queen,
my gaudy dear,
salt me a bird
and be its noose.
Bounce me off
like a shuttlecock.
Dance me dingo-sweet
for I am your lizard,
your sly thing.

Long ago
there was a peasant
who was poor but crafty.
He was not yet a voyeur.
He had yet to find
the miller's wife
at her game.
Now he had not enough
cabbage for supper
nor clover for his one cow.
So he slaughtered the cow
and took the skin
to town.
It was worth no more

than a dead fly
but he hoped for profit.

On his way
he came upon a raven
with damaged wings.
It lay as crumpled as
a wet washcloth.
He said, Come little fellow,
you're part of my booty.

On his way
there was a fierce storm.
Hail jabbed the little peasant's cheeks
like toothpicks.
So he sought shelter at the miller's house.
The miller's wife gave him only
a hunk of stale bread
and let him lie down on some straw.
The peasant wrapped himself and the raven
up in the cowhide
and pretended to fall asleep.

When he lay
as still as a sausage
the miller's wife
let in the parson, saying,
My husband is out
so we shall have a feast.
Roast meat, salad, cakes and wine.
The parson,

his eyes as black as caviar,
said, Come, my lily,
my fringy queen.
The miller's wife,
her lips as red as pimentoes,
said, Touch me, my pancake,
and wake me up.
And thus they ate.
And thus
they dingoed-sweet.

Then the miller
was heard stomping on the doorstep
and the miller's wife
hid the food about the house
and the parson in the cupboard.

The miller asked, upon entering,
What is that dead cow doing in the corner?
The peasant spoke up.
It is mine.
I sought shelter from the storm.
You are welcome, said the miller,
but my stomach is as empty as a flour sack.
His wife told him she had no food
but bread and cheese.
So be it, the miller said,
and the three of them ate.

The miller looked once more

at the cowskin
and asked its purpose.
The peasant answered,
I hide my soothsayer in it.
He knows five things about you
but the fifth he keeps to himself.
The peasant pinched the raven's head
and it croaked, Krr. Krr.
That means, translated the peasant,
there is wine under the pillow.
And there it sat
as warm as a specimen.

Krr. Krr.
They found the roast meat under the stove.
It lay there like an old dog.
Krr. Krr.
They found the salad in the bed
and the cakes under it.
Krr. Krr.

Because of all this
the miller burned to know the fifth thing.
How much? he asked,
little caring he was being milked.
They settled on a large sum
and the soothsayer said,
The devil is in the cupboard.
And the miller unlocked it.
Krr. Krr.

There stood the parson,
rigid for a moment,
as real as a soup can
and then he took off like a fire
with the wind at its back.
I have tricked the devil,
cried the miller with delight,
and I have tweaked his chin whiskers.
I will be as famous as the king.

The miller's wife
smiled to herself.
Though never again to dingo-sweet
her secret was as safe
as a fly in an outhouse.

The sly little peasant
strode home the next morning,
a soothsayer over his shoulder
and gold pieces knocking like marbles
in his deep pants pocket.
Krr. Krr.

GODFATHER DEATH

Hurry, Godfather death,
Mister tyranny,
each message you give
has a dance to it,
a fish twitch,
a little crotch dance.

A man, say,
has twelve children
and damns the next
at the christening ceremony.
God will not be the godfather,
that skeleton wearing his bones like a broiler,
or his righteousness like a swastika.
The devil will not be the godfather
wearing his streets like a whore.
Only death with its finger on our back
will come to the ceremony.

Death, with a one-eyed jack in his hand,
makes a promise to the thirteenth child:
My Godchild, physician you will be,

the one wise one, the one never wrong,
taking your cue from me.
When I stand at the head of the dying man,
he will die indelicately and come to me.
When I stand at his feet,
he will run on the glitter of wet streets once more.
And so it came to be.

Thus this doctor was never a beginner.
He knew who would go.
He knew who would stay.
This doctor,
this thirteenth but chosen,
cured on straw or midocean.
He could not be elected.
He was not the mayor.
He was more famous than the king.
He peddled his fingernails for gold
while the lepers turned into princes.

His wisdom
outnumbered him
when the dying king called him forth.
Godfather death stood by the head
and the jig was up.
This doctor,
this thirteenth but chosen,
swiveled that king like a shoebox
from head to toe,
and so, my dears,
he lived.

Godfather death replied to this:
Just once I'll shut my eyelid,
you blundering cow.
Next time, Godchild,
I'll rap you under my ankle
and take you with me.
The doctor agreed to that.
He thought: A dog only laps lime once.

It came to pass,
however,
that the king's daughter was dying.
The king offered his daughter in marriage
if she were to be saved.
The day was as dark as the Führer's headquarters.
Godfather death stood once more at the head.
The princess was as ripe as a tangerine.
Her breasts purred up and down like a cat.
I've been bitten! I've been bitten!
cried the thirteenth but chosen
who had fallen in love
and thus turned her around like a shoebox.

Godfather death
turned him over like a camp chair
and fastened a rope to his neck
and led him into a cave.
In this cave, murmured Godfather death,
all men are assigned candles
that inch by inch number their days.

Your candle is here.
And there it sat,
no bigger than an eyelash.
The thirteenth but chosen
jumped like a wild rabbit on a hook
and begged it be relit.
His white head hung out like a carpet bag
and his crotch turned blue as a blood blister,
and Godfather death, as it is written,
put a finger on his back
for the big blackout,
the big no.

RAPUNZEL

A woman
who loves a woman
is forever young.
The mentor
and the student
feed off each other.
Many a girl
had an old aunt
who locked her in the study
to keep the boys away.
They would play rummy
or lie on the couch
and touch and touch.
Old breast against young breast . . .

Let your dress fall down your shoulder,
come touch a copy of you
for I am at the mercy of rain,
for I have left the three Christs of Ypsilanti,
for I have left the long naps of Ann Arbor
and the church spires have turned to stumps.
The sea bangs into my cloister

for the young politicians are dying,
are dying so hold me, my young dear,
hold me . . .

The yellow rose will turn to cinder
and New York City will fall in

before we are done so hold me,
my young dear, hold me.
Put your pale arms around my neck.
Let me hold your heart like a flower
lest it bloom and collapse.
Give me your skin
as sheer as a cobweb,
let me open it up
and listen in and scoop out the dark.
Give me your nether lips
all puffy with their art
and I will give you angel fire in return.
We are two clouds
glistening in the bottle glass.
We are two birds
washing in the same mirror.
We were fair game
but we have kept out of the cesspool.
We are strong.
We are the good ones.
Do not discover us
for we lie together all in green
like pond weeds.
Hold me, my young dear, hold me.

They touch their delicate watches
one at a time.
They dance to the lute
two at a time.
They are as tender as bog moss.

They play mother-me-do
all day.
A woman
who loves a woman
is forever young.

Once there was a witch's garden
more beautiful than Eve's
with carrots growing like little fish,
with many tomatoes rich as frogs,
onions as ingrown as hearts,
the squash singing like a dolphin
and one patch given over wholly to magic —
rampion, a kind of salad root,
a kind of harebell more potent than penicillin,
growing leaf by leaf, skin by skin,
as rapt and as fluid as Isadora Duncan.
However the witch's garden was kept locked
and each day a woman who was with child
looked upon the rampion wildly,
fancying that she would die
if she could not have it.
Her husband feared for her welfare
and thus climbed into the garden
to fetch the life-giving tubers.

Ah ha, cried the witch,
whose proper name was Mother Gothel,
you are a thief and now you will die.

However they made a trade,
typical enough in those times.
He promised his child to Mother Gothel
so of course when it was born
she took the child away with her.
She gave the child the name Rapunzel,
another name for the life-giving rampion.
Because Rapunzel was a beautiful girl
Mother Gothel treasured her beyond all things.
As she grew older Mother Gothel thought:
None but I will ever see her or touch her.
She locked her in a tower without a door
or a staircase. It had only a high window.
When the witch wanted to enter she cried:
Rapunzel, Rapunzel, let down your hair.
Rapunzel's hair fell to the ground like a rainbow.
It was as yellow as a dandelion
and as strong as a dog leash.
Hand over hand she shinnied up
the hair like a sailor
and there in the stone-cold room,
as cold as a museum,
Mother Gothel cried:
Hold me, my young dear, hold me,
and thus they played mother-me-do.

Years later a prince came by
and heard Rapunzel singing in her loneliness.
That song pierced his heart like a valentine
but he could find no way to get to her.

Like a chameleon he hid himself among the trees
and watched the witch ascend the swinging hair.
The next day he himself called out:
Rapunzel, Rapunzel, let down your hair,
and thus they met and he declared his love.
What is this beast, she thought,
with muscles on his arms
like a bag of snakes?
What is this moss on his legs?
What prickly plant grows on his cheeks?
What is this voice as deep as a dog?
Yet he dazzled her with his answers.
Yet he dazzled her with his dancing stick.
They lay together upon the yellowy threads,
swimming through them
like minnows through kelp
and they sang out benedictions like the Pope.

Each day he brought her a skein of silk
to fashion a ladder so they could both escape.
But Mother Gothel discovered the plot
and cut off Rapunzel's hair to her ears
and took her into the forest to repent.
When the prince came the witch fastened
the hair to a hook and let it down.
When he saw that Rapunzel had been banished
he flung himself out of the tower, a side of beef.
He was blinded by thorns that pricked him like tacks.
As blind as Oedipus he wandered for years
until he heard a song that pierced his heart

like that long-ago valentine.
As he kissed Rapunzel her tears fell on his eyes
and in the manner of such cure-alls
his sight was suddenly restored.

They lived happily as you might expect
proving that mother-me-do
can be outgrown,
just as the fish on Friday,
just as a tricycle.
The world, some say,
is made up of couples.
A rose must have a stem.

As for Mother Gothel,
her heart shrank to the size of a pin,
never again to say: Hold me, my young dear,
hold me,
and only as she dreamt of the yellow hair
did moonlight sift into her mouth.

IRON HANS

Take a lunatic
for instance,
with Saint Averton, the patron saint,
a lunatic wearing that strait jacket
like a sleeveless sweater,
singing to the wall like Muzak,
how he walks east to west,
west to east again
like a fish in an aquarium.
And if they stripped him bare
he would fasten his hands around your throat.
After that he would take your corpse
and deposit his sperm in three orifices.
You know, I know,
you'd run away.

I am mother of the insane.
Let me give you my children:

Take a girl sitting in a chair
like a china doll.
She doesn't say a word.

She doesn't even twitch.
She's as still as furniture.
And you'll move off.

Take a man who is crying
over and over,
his face like a sponge.
You'll move off.

Take a woman talking,
purging herself with rhymes,
drumming words out like a typewriter,
planting words in you like grass seed.
You'll move off.

Take a man full of suspicions
saying: Don't touch this,
you'll be electrocuted.
Wipe off this glass three times.
There is arsenic in it.
I hear messages from God
through the fillings in my teeth.

Take a boy on a bridge.
One hundred feet up. About to jump,
thinking: This is my last ball game.
This time it's a home run.
Wanting the good crack of the bat.
Wanting to throw his body away
like a corn cob.
And you'll move off.

Take an old lady in a cafeteria
staring at the meat loaf,
crying: Mama! Mama!
And you'll move off.

Take a man in a cage
wetting his pants,
beating on that crib,
breaking his iron hands in two.
And you'll move off.

Clifford, Vincent, Friedrich,
my scooter boys,
deep in books,
long before you were mad.
Zelda, Hannah, Renée.
Moon girls,
where did you go?

There once was a king
whose forest was bewitched.
All the huntsmen,
all the hounds,
disappeared in it like soap bubbles.
A brave huntsman and his dog
entered one day to test it.
The dog drank from a black brook;
as he lapped an arm reached out
and pulled him under.
The huntsman emptied the pool
pail by pail by pail

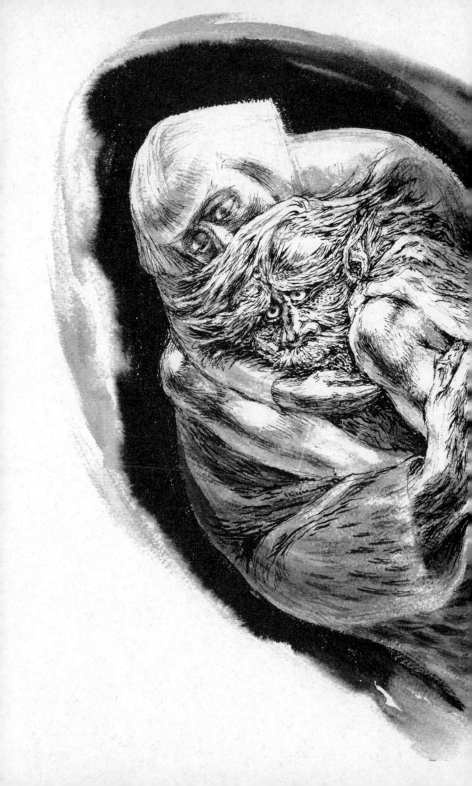

and at the bottom lay
a wild man,
his body rusty brown.
His hair covering his knees.
Perhaps he was no more dangerous
than a hummingbird;
perhaps he was Christ's boy-child;
perhaps he was only bruised like an apple
but he appeared to them to be a lunatic.
The king placed him in a large iron cage
in the courtyard of his palace.
The court gathered around the wild man
and munched peanuts and sold balloons
and not until he cried out:
Agony! Agony!
did they move off.

The king's son
was playing with his ball one day
and it rolled into the iron cage.
It appeared as suddenly as a gallstone.
The wild man did not complain.
He talked calmly to the boy
and convinced him to unlock the cage.
The wild man carried him and his ball
piggyback off into the woods
promising him good luck and gold for life.

The wild man set the boy at a golden spring
and asked him to guard it from a fox

or a feather that might pollute it.
The boy agreed and took up residence there.
The first night he dipped his finger in.
It turned to gold; as gold as a fountain pen,
but the wild man forgave him.
The second night he bent to take a drink
and his hair got wet, turning as gold
as Midas' daughter.
As stiff as the Medusa hair of a Greek statue.
This time the wild man could not forgive him.
He sent the boy out into the world.
But if you have great need, he said,
you may come into the forest and call *Iron Hans*
and I will come to help you for you
were the only one who was kind
to this accursed bull of a wild man.

The boy went out into the world,
his gold hair tucked under a cap.
He found work as a gardener's boy
at a far-off castle. All day set out
under the red ball to dig and weed.
One day he picked some wildflowers
for the princess and took them to her.
She demanded he take off his cap
in her presence. You look like a jester,
she taunted him, but he would not.
You look like a bird, she taunted him,
and snatched off the cap.
His hair fell down with a clang.

It fell down like a moon chain
and it delighted her.
The princess fell in love.

Next there was a war
that the king was due to lose.
The boy went into the forest
and called out: Iron Hans, Iron Hans,
and the wild man appeared.
He gave the boy a black charger,
a sword as sharp as a guillotine
and a great body of black knights.
They went forth and cut the enemy down
like a row of cabbage heads.
Then they vanished.
The court talked of nothing
but the unknown knight in a cap.
The princess thought of the boy
but the head gardener said:
Not he. He had only a three-legged horse.
He could have done better with a stork.
Three days in a row,
the princess, hoping to lure him back,
threw a gold ball.
Remember back,
the boy was good at losing balls
but was he good at catching them?
Three days running the boy,
thanks to Iron Hans,
performed like Joe Dimaggio.

And thus they were married.

At the wedding feast
the music stopped suddenly
and a door flew open
and a proud king walked in
and embraced the boy.
Of course
it was Iron Hans.
He had been bewitched
and the boy had broken the spell.
He who slays the warrior
and captures the maiden's heart
undoes the spell.
He who kills his father
and thrice wins his mother
undoes the spell.

Without Thorazine
or benefit of psychotherapy
Iron Hans was transformed.
No need for Master Medical;
no need for electroshock —
merely bewitched all along.
Just as the frog who was a prince.
Just as the madman his simple boyhood.

When I was a wild man,
Iron Hans said,
I tarnished all the world.

I was the infector.
I was the poison breather.
I was a professional,
but you have saved me
from the awful babble
of that calling.

CINDERELLA

You always read about it:
the plumber with twelve children
who wins the Irish Sweepstakes.
From toilets to riches.
That story.

Or the nursemaid,
some luscious sweet from Denmark
who captures the oldest son's heart.
From diapers to Dior.
That story.

Or a milkman who serves the wealthy,
eggs, cream, butter, yogurt, milk,
the white truck like an ambulance
who goes into real estate
and makes a pile.
From homogenized to martinis at lunch.

Or the charwoman
who is on the bus when it cracks up
and collects enough from the insurance.

From mops to Bonwit Teller.
That story.

Once
the wife of a rich man was on her deathbed
and she said to her daughter Cinderella:
Be devout. Be good. Then I will smile
down from heaven in the seam of a cloud.
The man took another wife who had
two daughters, pretty enough
but with hearts like blackjacks.
Cinderella was their maid.
She slept on the sooty hearth each night
and walked around looking like Al Jolson.
Her father brought presents home from town,
jewels and gowns for the other women
but the twig of a tree for Cinderella.
She planted that twig on her mother's grave
and it grew to a tree where a white dove sat.
Whenever she wished for anything the dove
would drop it like an egg upon the ground.
The bird is important, my dears, so heed him.

Next came the ball, as you all know.
It was a marriage market.
The prince was looking for a wife.
All but Cinderella were preparing
and gussying up for the big event.
Cinderella begged to go too.
Her stepmother threw a dish of lentils

into the cinders and said: Pick them
up in an hour and you shall go.
The white dove brought all his friends;
all the warm wings of the fatherland came,
and picked up the lentils in a jiffy.
No, Cinderella, said the stepmother,
you have no clothes and cannot dance.
That's the way with stepmothers.

Cinderella went to the tree at the grave
and cried forth like a gospel singer:
Mama! Mama! My turtledove,
send me to the prince's ball!
The bird dropped down a golden dress
and delicate little gold slippers.
Rather a large package for a simple bird.
So she went. Which is no surprise.
Her stepmother and sisters didn't
recognize her without her cinder face
and the prince took her hand on the spot
and danced with no other the whole day.

As nightfall came she thought she'd better
get home. The prince walked her home
and she disappeared into the pigeon house
and although the prince took an axe and broke
it open she was gone. Back to her cinders.
These events repeated themselves for three days.
However on the third day the prince
covered the palace steps with cobbler's wax
and Cinderella's gold shoe stuck upon it.

Now he would find whom the shoe fit
and find his strange dancing girl for keeps.
He went to their house and the two sisters
were delighted because they had lovely feet.
The eldest went into a room to try the slipper on
but her big toe got in the way so she simply
sliced it off and put on the slipper.
The prince rode away with her until the white dove
told him to look at the blood pouring forth.
That is the way with amputations.
They don't just heal up like a wish.
The other sister cut off her heel
but the blood told as blood will.
The prince was getting tired.
He began to feel like a shoe salesman.
But he gave it one last try.
This time Cinderella fit into the shoe
like a love letter into its envelope.

At the wedding ceremony
the two sisters came to curry favor
and the white dove pecked their eyes out.
Two hollow spots were left
like soup spoons.

Cinderella and the prince
lived, they say, happily ever after,
like two dolls in a museum case
never bothered by diapers or dust,
never arguing over the timing of an egg,

never telling the same story twice,
never getting a middle-aged spread,
their darling smiles pasted on for eternity.
Regular Bobbsey Twins.
That story.

ONE-EYE, TWO-EYES, THREE-EYES

Even in the pink crib
the somehow deficient,
the somehow maimed,
are thought to have
a special pipeline to the mystical,
the faint smell of the occult,
a large ear on the God-horn.

Still,
the parents have bizarre thoughts,
thoughts like a skill saw.
They accuse: Your grandfather,
your bad sperm, your evil ovary.
Thinking: The devil has put his finger upon us.
And yet in time
they consult their astrologer
and admire their trophy.
They turn a radish into a ruby.
They plan an elaborate celebration.
They warm to their roles.
They carry it off with a positive fervor.

The bird who cannot fly
is left like a cockroach.
A three-legged kitten is carried
by the scruff of the neck
and dropped into a blind cellar hole.
A malformed foal would not be nursed.
Nature takes care of nature.

I knew a child once
With the mind of a hen.
She was the favored one
for she was as innocent as a snowflake
and was a great lover of music.
She could have been a candidate
for the International Bach Society
but she was only a primitive.
A harmonica would do.
Love grew around her like crabgrass.
Even though she might live to the age of fifty
her mother planned a Mass of the Angels
and wore her martyrdom
like a string of pearls.

The unusual needs to be commented upon . . .
The Thalidomide babies
with flippers at their shoulders,
wearing their mechanical arms
like derricks.
The club-footed boy
wearing his shoe like a flat iron.

The idiot child,
a stuffed doll who can only masturbate.
The hunchback carrying his hump
like a bag of onions . . .
Oh how we treasure
their scenic value.

When a child stays needy until he is fifty —
oh mother-eye, oh mother-eye, crush me in —
the parent is as strong as a telephone pole.

Once upon a time
there were three sisters.
One with one eye
like a great blue aggie.
One with two eyes,
common as pennies.
One with three eyes,
the third like an intern.
Their mother loved only One-Eye and Three.
She loved them because they were God's lie.
And she liked to poke
at the unusual holes in their faces.
Two-Eyes was as ordinary
as an old man with a big belly
and she despised her.
Two-Eyes wore only rags
and ate only scraps from the dog's dish
and spent her days caring for their goat.

One day,
off in the fields with the goat
Two-Eyes cried, her cheeks as wet as a trout
and an old woman appeared before her
and promised if she sang to her goat
a feast would always be provided.
Two-Eyes sang and there appeared a table
as rich as one at Le Pavillon
and each dish bloomed like floribunda.
Two-Eyes, her eyes as matched as a pen and pencil set,
ate all she could.
This went on in a secret manner
until the mother and sisters saw
that she was not lapping from the dog dish.
So One-Eye came with her and her goat
to see where and how she got the secret food.
However Two-Eyes sang to her as softly as milk
and soon she fell fast asleep.
In this way Two-Eyes enjoyed her usual magic meal.
Next the mother sent Three-Eyes to watch.
Again Two-Eyes sang and again her sister fell asleep.
However her third eye did not shut.
It stayed as open as a clam on a half shell
and thus she witnessed the magic meal,
thus the mother heard all of it
and thus they killed the goat.

Again Two-Eyes cried like a trout
and again the old woman came to her
and told her to take some of the insides
of the slaughtered goat and bury them
in front of the cottage.
She carried forth the green and glossy intestine
and buried it where she was told.
The next morning they all saw
a great tree with leaves of silver
glittering like tinfoil
and apples made of fourteen carat gold.
One-Eye tried to climb up and pick one
but the branches merely withdrew.
Three-Eyes tried and the branches withdrew.
The mother tried and the branches withdrew.
May I try, said Two-Eyes,
but they replied:
You with your two eyes,
what can you do?
Yet when she climbed up and reached out
an apple came into her hand
as simply as a chicken laying her daily egg.

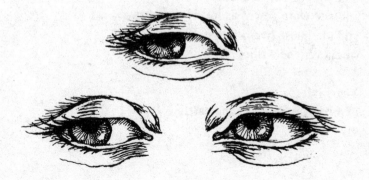

They bade her come down from the tree to hide
as a handsome knight was riding their way.
He stopped
and admired the tree
as you knew he would.
They claimed the tree as theirs
and he said sadly:
He who owns a branch of that tree
would have all he wished for in this world.
The two sisters clipped around the tree
like a pair of miming clowns
but not a branch or an apple came their way.
The tree treated them like poison ivy.
At last Two-Eyes came forth
and easily broke off a branch for him.

Quite naturally the knight carried her off
and the sisters were overjoyed
as now the tree would belong to them.
It burned in their brains like radium
but the next morning the tree had vanished.
The tree had, in the way of such magic,
followed Two-Eyes to the castle.
The knight married her
and she wore gowns as lovely as kisses
and ate goose liver and peaches
whenever she wished.

Years later
two beggars came to the castle,

along with the fishermen and the peasants
and the whole mournful lot.
These beggars were none other than her sisters
wearing their special eyes,
one the Cyclops,
one the pawnshop.
Two-Eyes was kind to them
and took them in
for they were magical.
They were to become her Stonehenge,
her cosmic investment,
her seals, her rings, her urns
and she became as strong as Moses.
Two-Eyes was kind to them
and took them in
because they were needy.
They were to become her children,
her charmed cripples, her hybrids —
oh mother-eye, oh mother-eye, crush me in.
So they took root in her heart
with their religious hunger.

THE WONDERFUL MUSICIAN

My sisters,
do you remember the fiddlers
of your youth?
Those dances
so like a drunkard
lighting a fire in the belly?
That speech,
as piercing as a loon's,
exciting both mayors
and cab drivers?
Sometimes,
ear to the bedside radio,
frozen on your cot
like a humped hairpin,
or jolt upright in the wind
on alternating current
like a fish on the hook
dancing the death dance,
remember
the vibrato,
a wasp in the ear?
Remember dancing in

those electric shoes?
Remember?
Remember music
and beware.

Consider
the wonderful musician
who goes quite alone
through the forest
and plays his fiddle-me-roo
to bring forth a companion.
The fox
was a womanly sort,
his tongue lapping a mirror.
But when he heard the music
he danced forth
in those electric shoes
and promised his life
if he too could learn to play.
The musician despised the fox
but nevertheless he said,
You have only to do as I bid you.
The fox replied,
I will obey you as
a scholar obeys his master.
Thus the musician
took him to an oak tree
and bade him put his left paw
in its wooden slit.
Then he fixed him with a wedge

until he was caught.
The fox was left there
kneeling like Romeo.

The musician went on
playing his fiddle-me-roo
to bring forth a companion.
The wolf,
a greedy creature,
his eye on the soup kettle,
heard the music
and danced forth
in those electric shoes.
He came forth
and was bilked
by the same order.
The musician fastened
both his paws to a hazel bush
and he hung spread-eagle
on a miniature crucifix.

The musician went on
playing his fiddle-me-roo
to bring forth a companion.
The hare,
a child of the dark,
his tail twitching
over the cellar hole,
came forth and was had.
With a rope around his throat

he ran twenty times around the maypole
until he foamed up
like a rabid dog.

The fox
as clever as a martyr
freed himself
and coming upon the crucifixion
and the rabid dog,
undid them
and all three swept
through the forest
to tear off the musician's
ten wonderful fingers.

The musician had gone on
playing his fiddle-me-roo.
Old kiteskin,
the bird,
had seen the persecution
and lay as still
as a dollar bill.
Old drowse-belly,
the snake,
did not come forth —
He lay as still as a ruler.
But a poor woodcutter
came forth with his axe
promising his life
for that music.

The wolf, the fox,
and the hare
came in for the kill.
The woodcutter
held up his axe —
it glinted like a steak knife —
and forecast their death.
They scuttled back into the wood
and the musician played
fiddle-me-roo
once more.
Saved by his gift
like many of us —
little Eichmanns,
little mothers —
I'd say.

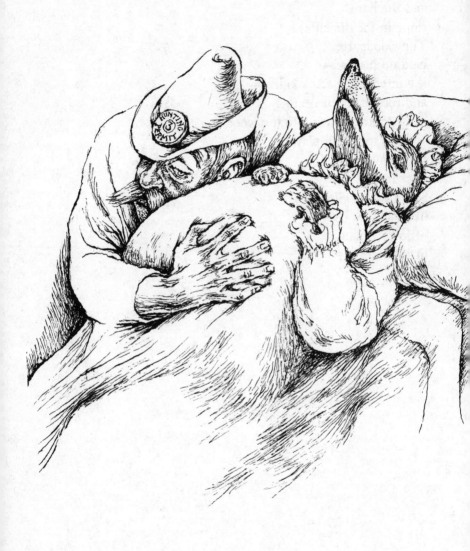

RED RIDING HOOD

Many are the deceivers:

The suburban matron,
proper in the supermarket,
list in hand so she won't suddenly fly,
buying her Duz and Chuck Wagon dog food,
meanwhile ascending from earth,
letting her stomach fill up with helium,
letting her arms go loose as kite tails,
getting ready to meet her lover
a mile down Apple Crest Road
in the Congregational Church parking lot.

Two seemingly respectable women
come up to an old Jenny
and show her an envelope
full of money
and promise to share the booty
if she'll give them ten thou
as an act of faith.
Her life savings are under the mattress
covered with rust stains

and counting.
They are as wrinkled as prunes
but negotiable.
The two women take the money and disappear.
Where is the moral?
Not all knives are for
stabbing the exposed belly.
Rock climbs on rock
and it only makes a seashore.
Old Jenny has lost her belief in mattresses
and now she has no wastebasket in which
to keep her youth.

The standup comic
on the "Tonight" show
who imitates the Vice President
and cracks up Johnny Carson
and delays sleep for millions
of bedfellows watching between their feet,
slits his wrist the next morning
in the Algonquin's old-fashioned bathroom,
the razor in his hand like a toothbrush,
wall as anonymous as a urinal,
the shower curtain his slack rubberman audience,
and then the slash
as simple as opening a letter
and the warm blood breaking out like a rose
upon the bathtub with its claw and ball feet.

And I. I too.
Quite collected at cocktail parties,

meanwhile in my head
I'm undergoing open-heart surgery.
The heart, poor fellow,
pounding on his little tin drum
with a faint death beat.
The heart, that eyeless beetle,
enormous that Kafka beetle,
running panicked through his maze,
never stopping one foot after the other
one hour after the other
until he gags on an apple
and it's all over.

And I. I too again.
I built a summer house on Cape Ann.
A simple A-frame and this too was
a deception — nothing haunts a new house.
When I moved in with a bathing suit and tea bags
the ocean rumbled like a train backing up
and at each window secrets came in
like gas. My mother, that departed soul,
sat in my Eames chair and reproached me
for losing her keys to the old cottage.
Even in the electric kitchen there was
the smell of a journey. The ocean
was seeping through its frontiers
and laying me out on its wet rails.
The bed was stale with my childhood
and I could not move to another city
where the worthy make a new life.

Long ago
there was a strange deception:
a wolf dressed in frills,
a kind of transvestite.
But I get ahead of my story.
In the beginning
there was just little Red Riding Hood,
so called because her grandmother
made her a red cape and she was never without it.
It was her Linus blanket, besides
it was red, as red as the Swiss flag,
yes it was red, as red as chicken blood.
But more than she loved her riding hood
she loved her grandmother who lived
far from the city in the big wood.

This one day her mother gave her
a basket of wine and cake
to take to her grandmother
because she was ill.
Wine and cake?
Where's the aspirin? The penicillin?
Where's the fruit juice?
Peter Rabbit got camomile tea.
But wine and cake it was.

On her way in the big wood
Red Riding Hood met the wolf.
Good day, Mr. Wolf, she said,
thinking him no more dangerous

than a streetcar or a panhandler.
He asked where she was going
and she obligingly told him.
There among the roots and trunks
with the mushrooms pulsing inside the moss
he planned how to eat them both,
the grandmother an old carrot
and the child a shy budkin
in a red red hood.
He bade her to look at the bloodroot,
the small bunchberry and the dogtooth
and pick some for her grandmother.
And this she did.
Meanwhile he scampered off
to Grandmother's house and ate her up
as quick as a slap.
Then he put on her nightdress and cap
and snuggled down into the bed.
A deceptive fellow.

Red Riding Hood
knocked on the door and entered
with her flowers, her cake, her wine.
Grandmother looked strange,
a dark and hairy disease it seemed.
Oh Grandmother, what big ears you have,
ears, eyes, hands and then the teeth.
The better to eat you with, my dear.
So the wolf gobbled Red Riding Hood down
like a gumdrop. Now he was fat.

He appeared to be in his ninth month
and Red Riding Hood and her grandmother
rode like two Jonahs up and down with
his every breath. One pigeon. One partridge.

He was fast asleep,
dreaming in his cap and gown,
wolfless.
Along came a huntsman who heard
the loud contented snores
and knew that was no grandmother.
He opened the door and said,
So it's you, old sinner.
He raised his gun to shoot him
when it occurred to him that maybe
the wolf had eaten up the old lady.
So he took a knife and began cutting open
the sleeping wolf, a kind of caesarian section.

It was a carnal knife that let
Red Riding Hood out like a poppy,
quite alive from the kingdom of the belly.
And grandmother too
still waiting for cakes and wine.
The wolf, they decided, was too mean
to be simply shot so they filled his belly
with large stones and sewed him up.
He was as heavy as a cemetery
and when he woke up and tried to run off
he fell over dead. Killed by his own weight.
Many a deception ends on such a note.

The huntsman and the grandmother and Red Riding
   Hood
sat down by his corpse and had a meal of wine and
   cake.
Those two remembering
nothing naked and brutal
from that little death,
that little birth,
from their going down
and their lifting up.

THE MAIDEN
WITHOUT HANDS

Is it possible
he marries a cripple
out of admiration?
A desire to own the maiming
so that not one of us butchers
will come to him with crowbars
or slim precise tweezers?
Lady, bring me your wooden leg
so I may stand on my own
two pink pig feet.
If someone burns out your eye
I will take your socket
and use it for an ashtray.
If they have cut out your uterus
I will give you a laurel wreath
to put in its place.
If you have cut off your ear
I will give you a crow
who will hear just as well.
My apple has no worm in it!
My apple is whole!

Once
there was a cruel father
who cut off his daughter's hands
to escape from the wizard.
The maiden held up her stumps
as helpless as dog's paws
and that made the wizard
want her. He wanted to lap
her up like strawberry preserve.
She cried on her stumps
as sweet as lotus water,
as strong as petroleum,
as sure-fire as castor oil.
Her tears lay around her like a moat.
Her tears so purified her
that the wizard could not approach.

She left her father's house
to wander in forbidden woods,
the good, kind king's woods.
She stretched her neck like an elastic,
up, up, to take a bite of a pear
hanging from the king's tree.
Picture her there for a moment,
a perfect still life.
After all,
she could not feed herself
or pull her pants down
or brush her teeth.

She was, I'd say,

without resources.
The king spied upon her at
that moment of stretching up, up
and he thought,
Eeny, Meeny, Miny, Mo —
There but for the grace of —
I will take her for my wife.

And thus they were married
and lived together on a sugar cube.
The king had silver hands made for her.
They were polished daily and kept in place,
little tin mittens.
The court bowed at the sight of them from a distance.
The leisurely passerby stopped and crossed himself.
What a fellow he is, they said of the king,
and kept their lips pursed as for a kiss.
But that was not the last word
for the king was called to war.
Naturally the queen was pregnant
so the king left her in care of his mother.
Buy her a perambulator, he said,
and send me a message when my son is born.
Let me hear no catcalls
or see a burned mattress.
He was superstitious.
You can see his point of view.

When the son was born
the mother sent a message

but the wizard intercepted it,
saying, instead, a changeling was born.
The king didn't mind.
He was used to this sort of thing by now.
He said: Take care,
but the wizard intercepted it,
saying: Kill both;
then cut out her eyes and send them,
also cut out his tongue and send it;
I will want my proof.

The mother,
now the grandmother —
a strange vocation to be a mother at all —
told them to run off in the woods.
The queen named her son
Painbringer
and fled to a safe cottage in the woods.
She and Painbringer were so good in the woods
that her hands grew back.
The ten fingers budding like asparagus,
the palms as whole as pancakes,
as soft and pink as face powder.

The king returned to the castle
and heard the news from his mother
and then he set out for seven years in the woods
never once eating a thing,
or so he said,
doing far better than Mahatma Gandhi.

He was good and kind as I have already said
so he found his beloved.
She brought forth the silver hands.
She brought forth Painbringer
and he realized they were his,
though both now unfortunately whole.
Now the butchers will come to *me*,
he thought, for I have lost my luck.
It put an insidious fear in him
like a tongue depressor held fast
at the back of your throat.
But he was good and kind
so he made the best of it
like a switch hitter.

They returned to the castle
and had a second wedding feast.
He put a ring on her finger this time
and they danced like dandies.
All their lives they kept the silver hands,
polished daily,
a kind of purple heart,
a talisman,
a yellow star.

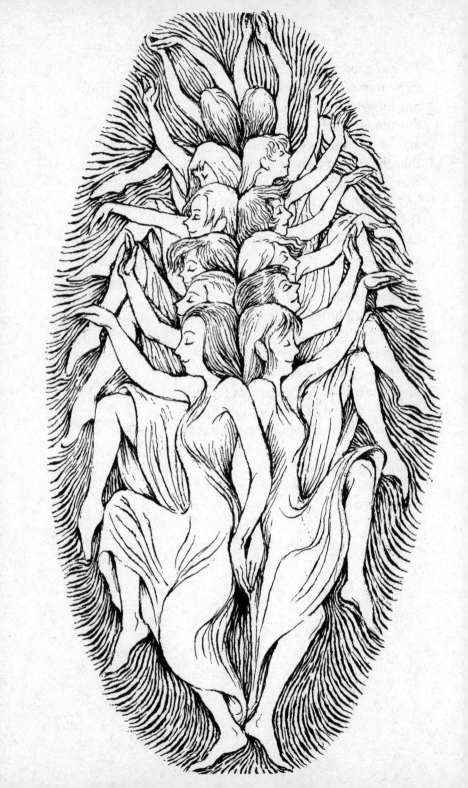

THE TWELVE DANCING
PRINCESSES

If you danced from midnight
to six A.M. who would understand?

The runaway boy
who chucks it all
to live on the Boston Common
on speed and saltines,
pissing in the duck pond,
rapping with the street priest,
trading talk like blows,
another missing person,
would understand.

The paralytic's wife
who takes her love to town,
sitting on the bar stool,
downing stingers and peanuts,
singing "That ole Ace down in the hole,"
would understand.

The passengers
from Boston to Paris

watching the movie with dawn
coming up like statues of honey,
having partaken of champagne and steak
while the world turned like a toy globe,
those murderers of the nightgown
would understand.

The amnesiac
who tunes into a new neighborhood,
having misplaced the past,
having thrown out someone else's
credit cards and monogrammed watch,
would understand.

The drunken poet
(a genius by daylight)
who places long-distance calls
at three A.M. and then lets you sit
holding the phone while he vomits
(he calls it "The Night of the Long Knives")
getting his kicks out of the death call,
would understand.

The insomniac
listening to his heart
thumping like a June bug,
listening on his transistor
to Long John Nebel arguing from New York,
lying on his bed like a stone table,
would understand.

The night nurse
with her eyes slit like Venetian blinds,
she of the tubes and the plasma,
listening to the heart monitor,
the death cricket bleeping,
she who calls you "we"
and keeps vigil like a ballistic missile,
would understand.

Once
this king had twelve daughters,
each more beautiful than the other.
They slept together, bed by bed
in a kind of girls' dormitory.
At night the king locked and bolted the door.
How could they possibly escape?
Yet each morning their shoes
were danced to pieces.
Each was as worn as an old jockstrap.
The king sent out a proclamation
that anyone who could discover
where the princesses did their dancing
could take his pick of the litter.
However there was a catch.
If he failed, he would pay with his life.
Well, so it goes.

Many princes tried,
each sitting outside the dormitory,
the door ajar so he could observe

what enchantment came over the shoes.
But each time the twelve dancing princesses
gave the snoopy man a Mickey Finn
and so he was beheaded.
Poof! Like a basketball.

It so happened that a poor soldier
heard about these strange goings on
and decided to give it a try.
On his way to the castle
he met an old old woman.
Age, for a change, was of some use.
She wasn't stuffed in a nursing home.
She told him not to drink a drop of wine
and gave him a cloak that would make
him invisible when the right time came.
And thus he sat outside the dorm.
The oldest princess brought him some wine
but he fastened a sponge beneath his chin,
looking the opposite of Andy Gump.

The sponge soaked up the wine,
and thus he stayed awake.
He feigned sleep however
and the princesses sprang out of their beds
and fussed around like a Miss America Contest.
Then the eldest went to her bed
and knocked upon it and it sank into the earth.
They descended down the opening
one after the other. The crafty soldier

put on his invisible cloak and followed.
Yikes, said the youngest daughter,
something just stepped on my dress.
But the oldest thought it just a nail.

Next stood an avenue of trees,
each leaf made of sterling silver.
The soldier took a leaf for proof.
The youngest heard the branch break
and said, Oof! Who goes there?
But the oldest said, Those are
the royal trumpets playing triumphantly.
The next trees were made of diamonds.
He took one that flickered like Tinkerbell
and the youngest said: Wait up! He is here!
But the oldest said: Trumpets, my dear.

Next they came to a lake where lay
twelve boats with twelve enchanted princes
waiting to row them to the underground castle.
The soldier sat in the youngest's boat
and the boat was as heavy as if an icebox
had been added but the prince did not suspect.

Next came the ball where the shoes did duty.
The princesses danced like taxi girls at Roseland
as if those tickets would run right out.
They were painted in kisses with their secret hair
and though the soldier drank from their cups
they drank down their youth with nary a thought.

Cruets of champagne and cups full of rubies.
They danced until morning and the sun came up
naked and angry and so they returned
by the same strange route. The soldier
went forward through the dormitory and into
his waiting chair to feign his druggy sleep.
That morning the soldier, his eyes fiery
like blood in a wound, his purpose brutal
as if facing a battle, hurried with his answer
as if to the Sphinx. The shoes! The shoes!
The soldier told. He brought forth
the silver leaf, the diamond the size of a plum.

He had won. The dancing shoes would dance
no more. The princesses were torn from
their night life like a baby from its pacifier.
Because he was old he picked the eldest.
At the wedding the princesses averted their eyes
and sagged like old sweatshirts.
Now the runaways would run no more and never
again would their hair be tangled into diamonds,
never again their shoes worn down to a laugh,
never the bed falling down into purgatory
to let them climb in after
with their Lucifer kicking.

THE FROG PRINCE

Frau Doktor,
Mama Brundig,
take out your contacts,
remove your wig.

I write for you.
I entertain.
But frogs come out
of the sky like rain.

Frogs arrive
With an ugly fury.
You are my judge.
You are my jury.

My guilts are what
we catalogue.
I'll take a knife
and chop up frog.

Frog has no nerves.
Frog is as old as a cockroach.

Frog is my father's genitals.
Frog is a malformed doorknob.
Frog is a soft bag of green.

The moon will not have him.
The sun wants to shut off
like a light bulb.
At the sight of him
the stone washes itself in a tub.
The crow thinks he's an apple
and drops a worm in.
At the feel of frog
the touch-me-nots explode
like electric slugs.

Slime will have him.
Slime has made him a house.

Mr. Poison
is at my bed.
He wants my sausage.
He wants my bread.

Mama Brundig,
he wants my beer.
He wants my Christ
for a souvenir.

Frog has boil disease
and a bellyful of parasites.

He says: Kiss me. Kiss me.
And the ground soils itself.

Why
should a certain
quite adorable princess
be walking in her garden
at such a time
and toss her golden ball
up like a bubble
and drop it into the well?
It was ordained.
Just as the fates deal out
the plague with a tarot card.
Just as the Supreme Being drills
holes in our skulls to let
the Boston Symphony through.

But I digress.
A loss has taken place.
The ball has sunk like a cast-iron pot
into the bottom of the well.

Lost, she said,
my moon, my butter calf,
my yellow moth, my Hindu hare.
Obviously it was more than a ball.
Balls such as these are not
for sale in Au Bon Marché.
I took the moon, she said,

between my teeth
and now it is gone
and I am lost forever.
A thief had robbed by day.

Suddenly the well grew
thick and boiling
and a frog appeared.
His eyes bulged like two peas
and his body was trussed into place.
Do not be afraid, Princess,
he said, I am not a vagabond,
a cattle farmer, a shepherd,
a doorkeeper, a postman
or a laborer.
I come to you as a tradesman.
I have something to sell.
Your ball, he said,
for just three things.
Let me eat from your plate.
Let me drink from your cup.
Let me sleep in your bed.
She thought, Old Waddler,
those three you will never do,
but she made the promises
with hopes for her ball once more.
He brought it up in his mouth
like a tricky old dog
and she ran back to the castle
leaving the frog quite alone.

That evening at dinner time
a knock was heard at the castle door
and a voice demanded:
King's youngest daughter,
let me in. You promised;
now open to me.
I have left the skunk cabbage
and the eels to live with you.
The king then heard of her promise
and forced her to comply.
The frog first sat on her lap.
He was as awful as an undertaker.
Next he was at her plate
looking over her bacon
and calves' liver.

We will eat in tandem,
he said gleefully.
Her fork trembled
as if a small machine
had entered her.
He sat upon the liver
and partook like a gourmet.
The princess choked
as if she were eating a puppy.
From her cup he drank.
It wasn't exactly hygienic.
From her cup she drank
as if it were Socrates' hemlock.

Next came the bed.
The silky royal bed.
Ah! The penultimate hour!
There was the pillow
with the princess breathing
and there was the sinuous frog
riding up and down beside her.
I have been lost in a river
of shut doors, he said,
and I have made my way over
the wet stones to live with you.
She woke up aghast.
I suffer for birds and fireflies
but not frogs, she said,
and threw him across the room.
Kaboom!

Like a genie coming out of a samovar,
a handsome prince arose in the
corner of her royal bedroom.
He had kind eyes and hands
and was a friend of sorrow.
Thus they were married.
After all he had compromised her.

He hired a night watchman
so that no one could enter the chamber
and he had the well
boarded over so that
never again would she lose her ball,
that moon, that Krishna hair,
that blind poppy, that innocent globe,
that madonna womb.

HANSEL AND GRETEL

Little plum,
said the mother to her son,
I want to bite,
I want to chew,
I will eat you up.
Little child,
little nubkin,
sweet as fudge,
you are my blitz.
I will spit on you for luck
for you are better than money.
Your neck as smooth
as a hard-boiled egg;
soft cheeks, my pears,
let me buzz you on the neck
and take a bite.
I have a pan that will fit you.
Just pull up your knees like a game hen.
Let me take your pulse
and set the oven for 350.
Come, my pretender, my fritter,
my bubbler, my chicken biddy!

Oh succulent one,
it is but one turn in the road
and I would be a cannibal!

Hansel and Gretel
and their parents
had come upon evil times.
They had cooked the dog
and served him up like lamb chops.
There was only a loaf of bread left.
The final solution,
their mother told their father,
was to lose the children in the forest.
We have enough bread for ourselves
but none for them.
Hansel heard this
and took pebbles with him
into the forest.
He dropped a pebble every fifth step
and later, after their parents had left them,
they followed the pebbles home.
The next day their mother gave them
each a hunk of bread
like a page out of the Bible
and sent them out again.
This time Hansel dropped bits of bread.
The birds, however, ate the bread
and they were lost at last.
They were blind as worms.
They turned like ants in a glove

not knowing which direction to take.
The sun was in Leo
and water spouted from the lion's head
but still they did not know their way.

So they walked for twenty days
and twenty nights
and came upon a rococo house
made all of food from its windows
to its chocolate chimney.
A witch lived in that house
and she took them in.
She gave them a large supper
to fatten them up
and then they slept,
z's buzzing from their mouths like flies.
Then she took Hansel,
the smarter, the bigger,
the juicier, into the barn
and locked him up.
Each day she fed him goose liver
so that he would fatten,
so that he would be as larded
as a plump coachman,
that knight of the whip.
She was planning to cook him
and then gobble him up
as in a feast
after a holy war.

She spoke to Gretel

and told her how her brother
would be better than mutton;
how a thrill would go through her
as she smelled him cooking;
how she would lay the table
and sharpen the knives
and neglect none of the refinements.
Gretel
who had said nothing so far
nodded her head and wept.
She who neither dropped pebbles or bread
bided her time.

The witch looked upon her
with new eyes and thought:
Why not this saucy lass
for an hors d'oeuvre?
She explained to Gretel
that she must climb into the oven
to see if she would fit.
Gretel spoke at last:
Ja, Fräulein, show me how it can be done.
The witch thought this fair
and climbed in to show the way.
It was a matter of gymnastics.
Gretel,
seeing her moment in history,
shut fast the oven,
locked fast the door,
fast as Houdini,

and turned the oven on to bake.
The witch turned as red
as the Jap flag.
Her blood began to boil up
like Coca-Cola.
Her eyes began to melt.
She was done for.
Altogether a memorable incident.

As for Hansel and Gretel,
they escaped and went home to their father.
Their mother,
you'll be glad to hear, was dead.
Only at suppertime
while eating a chicken leg
did our children remember
the woe of the oven,
the smell of the cooking witch,
a little like mutton,
to be served only with burgundy
and fine white linen
like something religious.

BRIAR ROSE
(SLEEPING BEAUTY)

Consider
a girl who keeps slipping off,
arms limp as old carrots,
into the hypnotist's trance,
into a spirit world
speaking with the gift of tongues.
She is stuck in the time machine,
suddenly two years old sucking her thumb,
as inward as a snail,
learning to talk again.
She's on a voyage.
She is swimming further and further back,
up like a salmon,
struggling into her mother's pocketbook.
Little doll child,
come here to Papa.
Sit on my knee.
I have kisses for the back of your neck.
A penny for your thoughts, Princess.
I will hunt them like an emerald.
Come be my snooky
and I will give you a root.

That kind of voyage,
rank as honeysuckle.

Once
a king had a christening
for his daughter Briar Rose
and because he had only twelve gold plates
he asked only twelve fairies
to the grand event.
The thirteenth fairy,
her fingers as long and thin as straws,
her eyes burnt by cigarettes,
her uterus an empty teacup,
arrived with an evil gift.
She made this prophecy:
The princess shall prick herself
on a spinning wheel in her fifteenth year
and then fall down dead.
Kaputt!
The court fell silent.
The king looked like Munch's *Scream*.
Fairies' prophecies,
in times like those,
held water.
However the twelfth fairy
had a certain kind of eraser
and thus she mitigated the curse
changing that death
into a hundred-year sleep.

The king ordered every spinning wheel
exterminated and exorcized.
Briar Rose grew to be a goddess
and each night the king
bit the hem of her gown
to keep her safe.
He fastened the moon up
with a safety pin
to give her perpetual light
He forced every male in the court
to scour his tongue with Bab-o
lest they poison the air she dwelt in.
Thus she dwelt in his odor.
Rank as honeysuckle.

On her fifteenth birthday
she pricked her finger
on a charred spinning wheel
and the clocks stopped.
Yes indeed. She went to sleep.
The king and queen went to sleep,
the courtiers, the flies on the wall.
The fire in the hearth grew still
and the roast meat stopped crackling.
The trees turned into metal
and the dog became china.
They all lay in a trance,
each a catatonic
stuck in the time machine.
Even the frogs were zombies.

Only a bunch of briar roses grew
forming a great wall of tacks
around the castle.
Many princes
tried to get through the brambles
for they had heard much of Briar Rose
but they had not scoured their tongues
so they were held by the thorns
and thus were crucified.
In due time
a hundred years passed
and a prince got through.
The briars parted as if for Moses
and the prince found the tableau intact.
He kissed Briar Rose
and she woke up crying:
Daddy! Daddy!
Presto! She's out of prison!
She married the prince
and all went well
except for the fear —
the fear of sleep.

Briar Rose
was an insomniac . . .
She could not nap
or lie in sleep
without the court chemist
mixing her some knock-out drops
and never in the prince's presence.

If it is to come, she said,
sleep must take me unawares
while I am laughing or dancing
so that I do not know that brutal place
where I lie down with cattle prods,
the hole in my cheek open.
Further, I must not dream
for when I do I see the table set
and a faltering crone at my place,
her eyes burnt by cigarettes
as she eats betrayal like a slice of meat.

I must not sleep
for while asleep I'm ninety
and think I'm dying.
Death rattles in my throat
like a marble.
I wear tubes like earrings.
I lie as still as a bar of iron.
You can stick a needle
through my kneecap and I won't flinch.
I'm all shot up with Novocain.
This trance girl
is yours to do with.
You could lay her in a grave,
an awful package,
and shovel dirt on her face
and she'd never call back: Hello there!
But if you kissed her on the mouth
her eyes would spring open

and she'd call out: Daddy! Daddy!
Presto!
She's out of prison.

There was a theft.
That much I am told.
I was abandoned.
That much I know.
I was forced backward.
I was forced forward.
I was passed hand to hand
like a bowl of fruit.
Each night I am nailed into place
and I forget who I am.
Daddy?
That's another kind of prison.
It's not the prince at all,
but my father
drunkenly bent over my bed,
circling the abyss like a shark,
my father thick upon me
like some sleeping jellyfish.

What voyage this, little girl?
This coming out of prison?
God help —
this life after death?